Basics

MW00714343

opening and closing loops and jump rings

1 Hold the jump ring with two pairs of chainnose pliers, or roundnose and chainnose pliers.

2 To open the jump ring, angle the tips of one pair of pliers toward you and angle the tips of the other pair away.

3 String materials on the open jump ring. Reverse the steps to close it.

making plain loops

1 Trim the wire ⅜ in. (1cm) above the top bead. Make a right-angle bend close to the bead.

2 Grab the tip of the wire with roundnose pliers. Roll the wire to form a half circle. Release the wire.

3 Reposition the pliers in the loop and continue rolling.

4 The finished loop should form a centered circle above the bead.

making wrapped loops

1 Make sure you have at least 1¼ in. (3.2cm) of wire above the bead. With the tip of chainnose pliers, grasp the wire directly above the bead. Bend the wire (above the pliers) into a right angle.

2 Using roundnose pliers, position the jaws vertically in the bend.

3 Bring the wire over the top jaw of the pliers.

4 Keep the jaws vertical and reposition the pliers' lower jaw snugly into the loop. Curve the wire downward around the bottom of the pliers. This is the first half of a wrapped loop.

5 Position the chainnose pliers' jaws across the loop.

6 Wrap the wire around the wire stem, covering the stem between the loop and the top of the bead. Trim the excess wire and press the cut end close to the wraps with chainnose or crimping pliers.

wrapping above a top-drilled bead

1 Center a top-drilled bead on a 3-in. (7.6cm) piece of wire. Bend each wire upward to form a squared-off "U" shape.

2 Cross the wires into an "X" above the bead.

3 Using chainnose pliers, make a small bend in each wire so the ends form a right angle.

4 Wrap the horizontal wire around the vertical wire as in a wrapped loop. Trim the excess wire. ✤

Head pin earrings

Make a wardrobe of earrings in a flash with a few beads, findings, and one easy technique. Your bead choice determines the style of this basic design—from elegant and refined to bold, delicate, or playful. With so many options, you may never buy earrings again.

1. String the desired beads on a head pin. Make a plain or a wrapped loop (Basics, p. 3) above the top bead.

2. Open the earring wire loop slightly and string it through the loop you just made. Close the loop. Make a second earring to match the first. ✤

Designed by the editors of BeadStyle.

Supply List

- **2** of each type of bead (4 if you use two of the same type on one earring)
- **2** head pins
- **2** earring wires
- roundnose and chainnose pliers
- diagonal wire cutters

Double dangles

Flower-shaped beads dangle gently from a strand of linked glass beads with delicate but dramatic results. Requiring only two easy techniques, these pretty and playful earrings are a breeze to make.

SupplyList

- **4** 9mm five-petal flower beads (Eclectica, 262-641-0910, eclecticabeads.com)
- **4** 4mm round crystals
- **4** seed beads, size 11º
- **4** 2½-in. (6.3cm) head pins
- **14** 4mm faceted glass beads
- 18 in. (46cm) 22-gauge sterling silver wire
- **2** 4mm jump rings
- **2** lever-back earring wires
- chainnose and roundnose pliers
- diagonal wire cutters

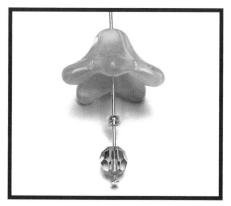

1. String a crystal, a seed bead, and a flower bead on a head pin. Depending on the shape of your flower, you might need more than one seed bead to extend the crystal beneath the flower.

2. Make a wrapped loop (Basics, p. 3) above the flower.

3. To make the glass bead units, cut 14 1¼ in. (3.2cm) pieces of wire. Turn a plain loop (Basics) at one end of a piece of wire. String a glass bead on the wire and turn a plain loop above the glass bead. Repeat with each remaining piece of wire. *Continued on the next page*

4. Open a loop on a glass bead unit (Basics) and link it to another glass bead unit. Close the loop. Attach one more bead unit and a flower unit.

Repeat to link four glass bead units and a flower unit.

5. Open a jump ring (Basics). Slide both dangles on the ring.

6. Slide the jump ring into the loop of the earring wire. Close the jump ring.

Repeat steps 4 through 6 to make a second earring the mirror image of the first. ❖

Designed by Linda Augsburg.
Contact her in care of BeadStyle.

Carnelian clusters

Add a little spice to your wardrobe with these sporty carnelian earrings. Myth has it that this reddish-orange gemstone generates happiness and confidence while also promoting creativity and bringing out hidden talents. As each dangle is attached with a wrapped loop, one thing is certain—you'll be happy and confident with your wrapped loop technique after completing this project. If you've never done wrapped loops before, be sure to practice with inexpensive craft or copper wire before attempting this design with precious metal wire.

1. Cut a 3-in. (7.6cm) piece of wire. Make a plain loop (Basics, p. 3) at one end and string on a nugget. Make the first half of a wrapped loop (Basics) below the nugget.

2. Cut one piece of chain with seven links (1¾ in./4.5cm) and one with five links (1¼ in./3.2cm). If using the long-and-short style of chain, as shown here, leave a short link on one end of each chain and a long link at the other end. Slide the short-link ends onto the loop below the nugget. Complete the wraps.

3. To make the dangles, string a seed bead, an oval bead, and a seed bead on a head pin. Make the first half of a wrapped loop above the bead. Make a total of 12 dangles.

4. String the loop of one dangle through the end link of the longer chain. Complete the wrap.

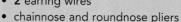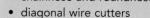

5. Attach a dangle on the left side of the next long link. Complete the wrap.

Supply**List**

- **2** 11 x 14mm faceted carnelian nuggets
- **24** 6mm oval carnelian beads
- 1g size 11º seed beads, complementary color
- 6 in. (15.2cm) long-and-short diamond chain, 3.5mm, gold filled
- **24** 1½-in. (3.8cm) 22-gauge head pins, gold filled
- 6 in. (15.2cm) 22-gauge wire, gold filled
- **2** earring wires
- chainnose and roundnose pliers
- diagonal wire cutters

6. Continue attaching dangles, alternating from the left side of one long link to the right side of the next long link. Continue this pattern until you have attached seven dangles.

Repeat steps 4 through 6 on the shorter chain, attaching five dangles.

7. Open the loop of an earring wire and string it through the loop above the carnelian nugget. Close the loop. Make a second earring to match the first. ❖

Designed by Paulette Biedenbender. Contact her in care of BeadStyle.

Spiral connections

Simple wire techniques highlight great beads. In the earrings shown at left, a small hammered spiral joins two sizes of textured raku beads from Fire in Belly (719-689-2388).

Remember—when any elements of your earrings have a direction (notice how the spirals look in the photo at left), assemble the components so they are mirror images of each other. That's the only way to get your earrings to hang correctly.

SupplyList

- **2** 15mm beads
- **2** 10mm beads
- 4 in. (10cm) 16-gauge wire
- 5 in. (13cm) 20-gauge wire or 3 in. (7.6cm) 20-gauge wire and **2** head pins
- **2** 3mm round beads
- **4** 5mm silver spacers
- **4** 4mm silver spacers
- **2** earring wires
- chainnose and roundnose pliers
- diagonal wire cutters
- ball peen hammer
- emery board or metal file, medium
- small anvil or bench block

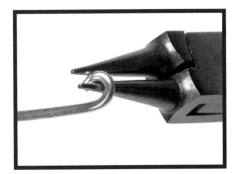

1. To start the spirals, cut two 2-in. (5cm) lengths of 16-gauge wire. Grab the end of one piece with the tip of your roundnose pliers and hold the other end with your fingers. Turn the pliers to form a small loop.

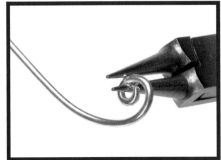

2. Continue turning the pliers, guiding the wire around the edge of the center loop to form a spiral. Make a second spiral with the other piece of wire.

3. Place one spiral on the anvil and hammer it gently to add texture. Hammer on one or both sides of each spiral.

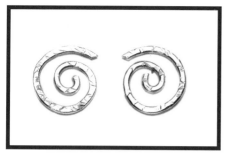

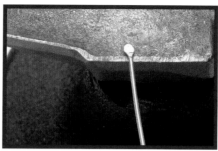

4. Before you hammer the second spiral, make sure you know which side to hit. The spirals should be mirror images of each other. Set the spirals aside.

5. If you're using purchased head pins, skip to step 6. To make your own head pins, cut two 1-in. (2.5cm) pieces of 20-gauge wire. Place the tip of one wire on the anvil and strike it firmly once or twice with the hammer. The end of the wire should flatten into a small paddle shape. Repeat with the other piece of wire. If the paddle edges are rough, smooth them with an emery board or metal file.

6. String a 4mm spacer, 10mm bead, and 4mm spacer on a head pin. Turn a plain loop above the top bead (Basics, p. 3). Make a second small-bead unit.

7. Cut two 1½-in. (3.8cm) lengths of 20-gauge wire. Turn a loop on one end of each wire. String a 5mm spacer, 15mm bead, 5mm spacer, and 3mm bead on each one. Turn another loop above each top bead.

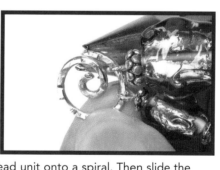

8. To connect the pieces, slide the small-bead unit onto a spiral. Then slide the large-bead unit's bottom loop (the end without the 3mm bead) onto the spiral. Gently squeeze the spiral closed with chainnose pliers. Make the second earring the mirror image of the first.

Designed by Wendy Witchner.
Contact her in care of BeadStyle.
See more of her work on her website,
wendywitchner-jewelry.com.

9. Open the loop on an earring wire and attach it to the top loop of one of the assembled earrings. Close the loop. Repeat with the second earring. ✤

Delicate chain earrings

Combine delicate silver chain with a few beads to make a pair of pretty, streamlined earrings. The earrings shown—Lucite butterflies and crystals dangled from varying lengths of chain—are perfect for a garden party or an evening out.

1. Cut a 2-, a 2¼-, and a 2¾-in. (5, 6, and 7cm) length of chain.

2. String two head pins with 4mm crystals and one with a butterfly bead and a crystal, as shown. Make the first half of a wrapped loop (Basics, p. 3) above each bead.

3. Slide each bead unit into the end link of the shorter chain segments. Attach the butterfly unit to the longest piece. Complete the wraps.

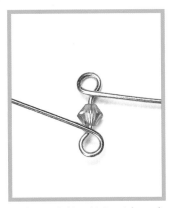

4. Cut a 2½-in. (6.3cm) length of 24-gauge wire. (Or use a head pin and snip off the head.) String a 3mm crystal and make the first half of a wrapped loop on each end.

5. On the bottom loop, string the three chain components from step 3. (String them from shortest to longest, as shown above, or put the longest component in the middle.) Complete the wraps on both loops.

6. Open the loop on an earring wire and attach the top loop of the bead unit to it.

7. Make a second earring the mirror image of the first. ✤

SupplyList

- 2 9 x 11mm Lucite butterfly beads
- 6 4mm bicone crystals, **2** each of three colors
- **2** 3mm bicone crystals
- 16 in. (41cm) fine-gauge cable chain
- 5 in. (13cm) 24-gauge wire or **2** 2½-in. (6.3cm) head pins
- 6 1½-in. (3.8cm) head pins
- 2 earring wires
- roundnose and chainnose pliers
- diagonal wire cutters

Designed by Naomi Fujimoto. Contact her in care of BeadStyle.

Fringed hoops

With an ever-increasing variety of earring findings available, why stop with the basics? This pair of earrings boasts tiny gemstones dangling in a funky fringe from hoop earrings with hanging loops. One technique—the handy plain loop—is all you need for success with this design. Don't forget to keep both your gemstones and your mood light.

1. String each rondelle, faceted round bead, and pearl on a head pin. Make a plain loop (Basics, p. 3) above each bead.

2. Open a loop on a dangle (Basics), attach it to an earring loop, and close the loop. Attach a second dangle to the same loop. Continue to attach pairs of dangles to each earring loop. Make a second earring to match the first. ✤

Supply List

- **28** or more 3-4mm gemstones or pearls, such as rondelles, faceted round beads, and button-shaped pearls
- **2** hoop earrings with hanging loops, approx. 27mm (Rio Grande, 800-545-6566)
- **28** or more 1-in. (2.5cm) decorative head pins
- chainnose and roundnose pliers
- diagonal wire cutters

Designed by Jill Italiano. Contact her at jill@bellaoro.com or view her collection at jillidesigns.com.

1. Cut two 3¾-in. (9.5cm) pieces of wire. With the tip of a pair of roundnose pliers, turn a small loop (Basics, p. 3) at one end of each.

2. Bend each wire at a right angle 1⅜ in. (3.5cm) from the top of the loop. Make a second right angle ⅜ in. (1cm) from the first.

3. Hammer the squared-off bottom section to flatten the wire and harden it. Don't hammer the sides past ⅛ in. (3mm) from the corners.

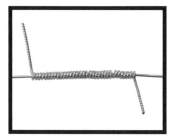

4. To make your own coiled wire spacers, wrap twisted wire around a 1-in. (2.5cm) segment of 20-gauge wire. Slide the coil off the wire core and cut it into four ¼-in. (6mm) sections.

5. String a 2.5mm bead, a coil or 6mm bead, a 3mm, an 8mm, a 3mm, a coil or 6mm, and a 2.5mm bead on each wire.

6. Slide the beads toward the flattened corner, as shown. Measure 1⅜ in. from the bottom, bend the wire's end at a right angle so it fits into the small loop, and trim it to ½ in. (1.3cm). Hammer the right angle as in step 3. Use a metal file or emery board to smooth the cut end. Finish the second earring to match the first. ❖

Right-angle earrings

Three right angles and a small loop define the basic shape of these simple earrings. Embellish them with silver or crystal beads as shown, or adapt this design to your own style by using gemstones, glass, or clay.

Designed by Wendy Witchner. Contact her in care of BeadStyle. See more of her work on her website, wendywitchner-jewelry.com.

SupplyList

- 8 in. (20cm) 20-gauge wire
- 1 ft. (31cm) 24-gauge twisted wire or 4 6mm beads
- 2 6-8mm beads
- 4 3mm round beads
- 4 2.5mm round beads
- chainnose and roundnose pliers
- emery board or metal file
- ball peen hammer
- small anvil or bench block
- diagonal wire cutters

Metal disk drops

Crystal dangles blend with metal elements to create earrings with great style and movement. Rounded, Eastern-inspired gold and silver disk findings take the lead, while colored crystals subtly accent these wear-anywhere earrings.

1. Place a main color (MC) crystal on a head pin. Trim the excess to ⅜ in. (1cm) and turn a loop above the crystal (Basics, p. 3). Make three more single-crystal units.

2. Place an MC crystal, a spacer, and an accent color (AC) crystal on a head pin. Trim the wire to ⅜ in. and make a loop above the last crystal. Make one more double-crystal unit.

3. If using wire instead of eye pins, cut the wire in half and make a loop at one end of each piece. String an MC crystal, a spacer, an AC crystal, and the disk finding on each eye pin (above left). Trim the excess wire to ⅜ in. and make a loop at the bottom (above right). *Continued on the next page*

4. Open the loop beneath each disk and slide on a single-crystal unit, a double-crystal unit, and a single-crystal unit. Close the loops.

5. Open the loop on the earring finding and slide the loop of the bead unit into it. Close the loop. Repeat to finish the second earring. ❖

Supply**List**

- **8** 4mm crystals, main color
- **4** 4mm crystals, accent color
- **4** metal spacers
- **2** 13mm disk-shaped findings
- **2** earring wires
- **6** 2-in. (5cm) head pins
- **2** 2-in. eye pins or
  5-in. (13cm) 20-gauge wire
- roundnose and chainnose pliers
- diagonal wire cutters

*Designed by Lea Rose Nowicki.
Contact her in care of BeadStyle.*

Chandelier-style earrings

Constructing chandelier-style earrings can be easier than you'd expect. Though not serving their intended purpose, the rings on these two-to-one findings work well for dangling beads in a trendy set of earrings. It's easy to adjust the length to suit your taste.

1. String a bead on a head pin, trim the wire to ⅜ in. (1cm) above the bead, and turn a plain loop (Basics, p. 3). Repeat to make 24 beaded head pins.

2. Cut a 1¼-in. (3.2cm) piece of wire and turn a plain loop at one end. String a bead on the wire. Trim the wire ⅜ in. above the bead and make a second plain loop. Repeat to make 26 plain-loop units.

3. Open a loop on a plain-loop unit (Basics) and link it through one of the bottom rings in the finding. Close the loop. Join a plain-loop unit to the other bottom ring and another to the center opening. Join a plain-loop unit to each of the outer plain-loop units.

Supply List

- **16-in.** (41cm) strand 4mm round beads, malachite
- **2** two-to-one connectors with a center opening
- **4** bar connectors
- **24** 1-in. (2.5cm) head pins
- **3** ft. (.91m) 22-gauge wire
- **2** earring wires
- chainnose and roundnose pliers
- diagonal wire cutters

4. Link the outer plain-loop units to the end rings of a bar connector. Connect a plain-loop unit to each end ring on the bar.

5. Connect the plain-loop units to the outer rings of another bar. (Place the bar pieces in the same direction.) Link two plain-loop units together and attach one pair to the center of the bottom bar and the other pairs to the outer rings on the bar.

6. Open the bottom loop of the top center unit and thread three beaded head pins on the loop. Close the loop. Repeat to add three beaded head pins to each of the bottom plain-loop units.

7. Open the loop of an earring wire, slide the top ring of the finding onto the earring wire, and close the loop. Make a second earring the mirror image of the first by flipping the bar connectors. ❖

Designed by Linda Augsburg. Contact her in care of BeadStyle.

Linked leaves

Leaf-shaped beads, in colors reminiscent of autumn leaves, are a natural selection for this design. Linking them together creates earrings that capture the idea of leaves falling gently to the ground. These earrings showcase a combination of three colors, but the design will work in a monochromatic color scheme as well.

1. Open a jump ring (Basics, p. 3), link it through a closed jump ring, and close it. Repeat to form a chain of eight rings. Repeat for the second earring.

2. Open 36 jump rings. String one leaf bead on each. Don't close the jump rings yet.

3. Connect two beaded jump rings to the bottom ring of one chain and close these rings. Work your way toward the top, adding one leaf to each side of each ring in the chain to keep the earring balanced.

Repeat on the second chain. You will have four beaded rings remaining. Close these rings.

SupplyList

- **52** or more 5mm jump rings
- Czech glass leaf-shaped beads (here **18** brown, **10** red, and **8** green)
- **2** 9 x 11mm round- or dome-shaped beads
- **2** earring wires
- 2½ in. (6.3cm) 20-gauge wire
- roundnose and chainnose pliers
- diagonal wire cutters

Joining beaded jump rings to linked rings is easier when the linked rings are suspended rather than flat. Slide a paper clip into the last ring and hang it on the hook of a banana holder or an ornament-hanging stand. This will bring the links to eye level, making it easier to see what you are doing.

4. Cut the wire in half. Make a small plain loop (Basics) on one end of each piece. String a dome-shaped bead on each wire and trim the wire to ⅜ in. (1cm) above the bead. Make a second plain loop.

5. Open the wire loop on the bottom of the bead unit. Slide on a beaded jump ring, the top link of chain, and another beaded jump ring. Close the loop.

6. Open the loop on the earring wire and slide the top loop of the bead unit onto it. Close the loop. Finish the second earring to match the first. ❖

Designed by Linda Augsburg. Contact her in care of BeadStyle.

Cascade earrings

Use connector bars as a starting point for these gorgeous cascades of beaded chain. Designing is a breeze when you attach all the chain segments first, then arrange the gemstone and crystal beads. Try summery watercolors in peridot, aquamarine, and tanzanite or muted fall hues of garnet, carnelian, and berry quartz.

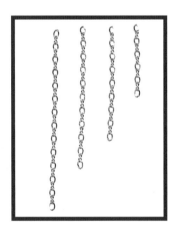

1. Cut pairs of chain segments in assorted lengths for each connector bar's hanging loop. (These range from 1¼–2¾ in./ 3.2–7cm.) Cut at least nine pairs. Reserve one segment from each pair for the second earring.

2. Open a jump ring (Basics, p. 3) and link it to one of the loops on the connector loop. Repeat for the other loops. String groupings of three or more segments of chain on each jump ring; close the jump rings.

3. String beads on head pins as desired and make the first half of a wrapped loop (Basics).

4. For top-drilled beads, cut a 2½-in. (6.3cm) piece of wire. String a bead and make a set of wraps above it (Basics).

Make the first half of a wrapped loop ⅛ in. (3mm) above the wraps.

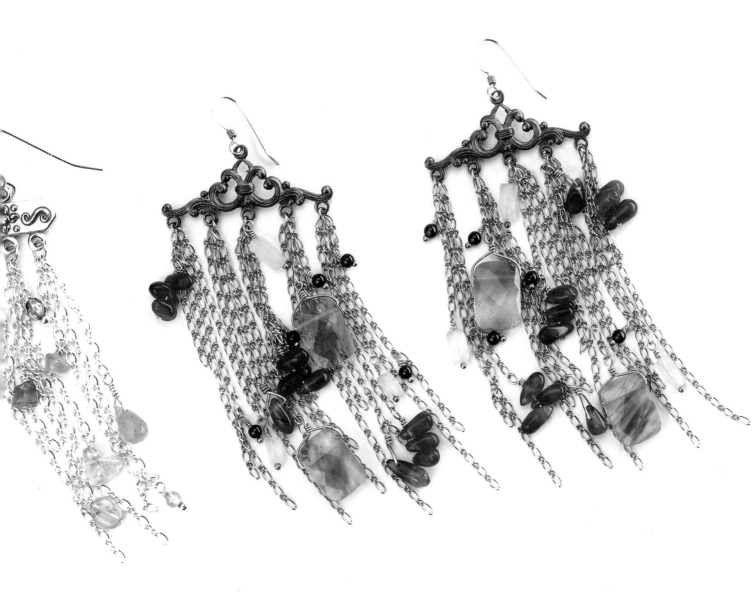

5. Attach dangles as desired, staggering their placement along each chain segment. When satisfied with the placement of the dangles, complete the wrapped loops.

6. Open the loop on an earring wire and attach the top loop of the connector bar. Close the earring wire loop.

Make a second earring the mirror image of the first, using the remaining chain segments. ❖

Supply List

quantities will vary
- 3-8 ft. (.91-2.44m) 2mm cable or figure-eight chain
- assorted 3-12mm gemstones and crystals
- **2** connector bars (gold bars from The Beadin' Path, 877-922-3237, beadinpath.com; silver bars from Rio Grande, 800-545-6566)
- 1½-in. (3.8cm) plain or decorative head pins
- 24-gauge wire, half hard
- 3-4mm jump rings
- **2** earring wires
- chainnose and roundnose pliers
- diagonal wire cutters

Designed by Brenda Schweder, who offers the gold earrings as a kit. Contact her at Miss Cellany Jewelry Kits, b@brendaschweder.com, or visit brendaschweder.com.

Get Great Jewelry Projects All Through the Year!

$1.99

867137
AO —
523 — G

No Exchange
Books
Crafts & Hobbies

35+ Fabulous jewelry projects • NEW LOGO, NEW LOOK

BEAD & BUTTON

Oct. 2004 • Issue 63
beadandbutton.com

Crochet a dramatic fall necklace

Beader's guide to gemstones
SPECIAL 4-PAGE PULLOUT

EXCITING NEW stitch combinations

For beginners
String an easy watch band

ELEGANT HOLIDAY ORNAMENTS
Get started now!

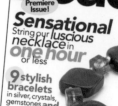

30+ Easy jewelry projects for today
Fast. Fashionable. Fun.

BeadStyle

Premiere Issue!

Sensational
String our luscious necklace in **one hour** or less

9 stylish bracelets in silver, crystals, gemstones and more!

3 simply fabulous pendant projects

Fun earrings for everyday

Your Beading Resource!

Bead&Button magazine

- New and traditional stitching techniques
- Fully-tested projects
- Step-by-step instructions and photos

Fast. Fashionable. Fun.

BeadStyle magazine

- Beautiful pieces in today's hottest styles
- Make jewelry in an evening or less
- Great photos and easy-to-follow instructions

If you enjoyed *Fast & Fashionable Earrings*, make sure you order these titles from the Easy-Does-It Series.

BEAD | 15 | Easy-Does-It Series
Easy Beaded Jewelry

BEAD | 11 PROJECTS | Easy-Does-It Series
Seed Bead Chains

BEAD | 15 PROJECTS | Easy-Does-It Series
Fun Beaded Earrings

BEAD | 7 PROJECTS | Easy-Does-It Series
Seed Bead Jewelry

BEAD | 28 PROJECTS | Easy-Does-It Series
Elegant Earrings

12286 CV4

Subscribe or Order Today and Enjoy
New Beading Projects Every Month!

Call 800-533-6644 or visit
beadandbuttonbooks.com

Kalmbach
PUBLISHING CO.

ISBN 0-89024-468-5 $7.95 U.S. 12286

90000>
9 780890 244685

0 64465 12286 8

AUDIO CD INCLUDED

Longman
English Interactive 4

Activity and
Resource Book

With Audio CD and Written Activities

Longman
longman.com

Michael Rost